Praise for
Poetry and Notes to Myself:
My Ups and Downs with A Course in Miracles
by Gerald G. Jampolsky, M.D.

"There are just a handful of people who had a direct relationship with the scribes of *A Course in Miracles*, who were there at the beginning and midwifed it into the world. They set the tone, laid the firm foundation, and thereby gave an inestimable gift to all of us who have been blessed by the teachings of the Course. Jerry Jampolsky is a teacher of the teachers, inspirer of inspirers, and shining light to all of us who have been fortunate enough to learn from his example. This book is one more demonstration of his extraordinary heart."

—Marianne Williamson, author of *Return to Love,*
Illuminata, The Law of Divine Compassion,
The Age of Miracles, The Gift of Change, Everyday Grace,
A Woman's Worth, and *Tears to Triumph*
www.marianne.com

"It is not uncommon for a six-year-old boy to say, "My Dad is my hero," believing he is superhuman and will never let him down. It is not so common for a sixty-year-old man to think of his father as his hero, but I do: Not because Dad lived up to my boyish fantasy, but because of how he has vulnerably and diligently lived his life in putting into practice *A Course in Miracles*. This book is his story, told through the beauty of poetry."

—Lee Jampolsky, Ph.D., author of *The Art of Trust,*
Listen to Me, Smile For No Good Reason, Healing Together,
Walking Through Walls, Healing the Addictive Personality,
and *How to Say Yes When Your Body Says No*
www.drleejampolsky.com

"Knowing Dr. Gerald Jampolsky for close to forty-five years, since my adolescence, I have had the privilege of witnessing a man who was overpoweringly interested in both the normal and paranormal universe, turn deeply within to a focused, committed interest in Attitudinal Healing, forgiveness and spirit. I watched a powerful yearning and diligent practice of *A Course in Miracles* transform this man, father figure and ultimately beloved friend, from a struggling, spiritually naïve and bereft being, into a profoundly wise and continually awakening sage. These poems return me to the time of Jerry's initiation into the spiritual and the humble beginnings of his transformative surrender to his true nature of love, that he so presently reflects for us all. They speak to the part in all of us that must begin somewhere in yearning and end somehow learning that we are all but love."

— Tamara Morgan, Co-President of the Foundation for Inner Peace, author of *Double Vision* with Judith Skutch Whitson
www.www.acim.org

&.

"I am honored to call Jerry Jampolsky a friend and teacher for nearly forty years. With the release of his first book, *Love is Letting Go of Fear*, he brought the powerful and seemingly complex message of *A Course in Miracles* to a world hungry for his practical and accessible message. With this new book, we are finding out how he moved from being a victim of the world to a place where love, forgiveness and healing became the way he walked in gratitude. I am inspired by his vim and vigor for learning, growing and sharing. He is a testament to the power of miracles to transform a life. I continue to be amazed by Jerry and Diane as they teach us all how to joyously and purposely walk home to God together."

—Beverly Hutchinson McNeff,
Co-Founder of Miracle Distribution Center
and Publisher of *The Holy Encounter*
www.miraclecenter.org

"In 2012, we assembled most of the peopl: who had translated *A Course in Miracles* into twenty-six forei n languages. At that meeting, Dr. Kenneth Wapnick warned all o 'us that studying and even translating the Course could bring o ly a superficial shift of consciousness. Only through the strug le to apply Course principles could a student hope to awaken to the awareness of Love's presence. In a validation of Ken's observation, Jerry's inspirational notes and poems testify to his struggle and rewards through the process of his personal awaker ing."

—William Whitson, Transla ions, Foundation for Inner Peace, author of *Test of B ttle: Born for Flight* and *Myths and Misinformation* www.acim.org

❧

"Dr. Jerry Jampolsky, who brought healin to countless people through his worldwide Centers for Attitudin l Healing, has served us up a delicious dessert! His new work, voven from love and wisdom, is spun from personal life stories, notes and poetry not made available till now. It serves as a guic ing light for all who seek truth. Its simplicity makes it an easy re d for all ages, and for anywhere you may be on the path. A beauti ul, poetic expression of spiritual principles and concepts. I highly ecommend it as a Joy to be read again and again in moments of so l searching and open hearts. Definitely a book to snuggle up with. '

—David Fishman, author of *Int Oneness, Thoughts and Prayers on the Way, The Open M nd: Loving Your Self* www.One MindFoundation.org

"Jerry takes us on an incredibly intimate journey of the soul. His words whisper to us: 'Come a little closer now, get to know me and love me. You are not alone. Open your heart - you are safe because I am you.'"

—Phoebe Lauren, J.D., author of *Space Between the Colors: How to Live When Your Child Dies, Beyond 'A Course in Miracles,' Star Child, I Am Sarah, The Golden Door, The Dance of Love,* and *Becoming Real* www.phoebelauren.com

☙

"Judy Whitson introduced me to Jerry Jampolsky M.D. in 1975 and he's been a wonderful friend ever since. In *Poetry and Notes to Myself*, Jerry has given us another gift of himself. Thank you, Jerry, for baring your soul and being willing to tell it all in such a poetic and loving way. There is a tremendous amount of honesty, openness and spiritual nuggets in this little book. I hope you'll take the time to taste this honey. I recommend it highly."

—Jon Mundy, Ph.D., publisher of *Miracles* magazine and author of *Living 'A Course in Miracles'* www.miraclesmagazine.org

☙

"We all know and admire Jerry - the master teacher of healing through love and forgiveness. This book reveals Jerry - the man by open display of his poetic soul."

—Jack and Eulalia Luckett

"Never was there a time that Jerry Jampolsky was not learning and growing and, in turn, teaching from his experience. I have known him almost sixty years and seen him at his worst. I have also seen him at his best. His recent book taps into the pain, the vulnerability, and the power of personal, spiritual transformation. With words that reach deep into the experiences of the heart and the mind, Jerry gifts us, once again, with his passionate poetry and prose."

—Paige Peterson, Executive Vice President
of the Huntsman Cancer Foundation
www.huntsmancancer.org/giving/foundation

ॐ

"Jerry's newest book, *Poetry and Notes to Myself: My Ups and Downs with A Course in Miracles*, is a testimony to the power of Spirit to release a willing heart from the ashes of darkness to the radiance of Love. Find comfort and reassurance in the notes of one soul's courageous inner journey."

—David Hoffmeister, author of *Unwind Your Mind Back to God*
www.awakening-mind.org

ॐ

"Jerry Jampolsky was one of the first *A Course In Miracles* students. He has been a steady fixture and a positive force in the ACIM movement since the beginning. His latest book *Poetry and Notes to Myself* puts together many of his deeply personal and profound writings in the form of poems, short essays and inspirational phrases so that his inspirations can now be our inspirations as well. Jerry is very revealing and honest in this latest work, as he finds the gems from forty plus years of self reflection and Course principle application. We are now all blessed to have this fine addition to his already amazing legacy of written works. Thank you Jerry."

— Rev. Tony Ponticello, Executive Minister
of Community Miracles Center (CMC)
and Publisher of CMC Miracles Monthly
www.miracles-course.org

"This collection of poetry and insightful vignettes, culled from over forty years of study with *A Course in Miracles*, is a personal and often intimate window into the life of one of the Course's earliest and most prominent practitioners. Yet its wisdom and heart will touch every reader. It may well be Jerry's finest work."

—Bob Rosenthal, M.D., Co-President of the Foundation for
Inner Peace and author of *From Plagues to Miracles*
www.acim.org

⚬

"Jerry Jampolsky's story is truly inspiring. He is a man whose life has been transformed by the application of the principles of *A Course in Miracles*, of which he was a pioneer. Many people will have read his wonderful books but be unaware that he has written powerful poetry as well. This book combines the two, in that Jerry tells his life story, through poems, written over many years – charting his passage from fear to love."

—Ian Patrick, Founder of Miracle Network in the UK
and Former Editor - Miracle Worker Magazine
www.miracles.org.uk

⚬

"If anyone should be considered a 'world treasure,' it's Jerry, and it is my deepest honor to offer tribute to this kind and generous man. He has been a towering example throughout the planet of single minded perseverance, of great trust in guidance, and of dedication to being helpful, to listening, to caring. To the four corners of the earth, Jerry and his soulmate and wife, Diane Cirincione, have taken the message of unconditional love and forgiveness, and in so doing, countless numbers of lives have been deeply enriched. They have left a trail of healing, comfort, and inspiration in every place they have visited.

"Jerry and I met thirty-nine years ago, and my life changed forever. As friends, colleagues, and fellow travelers on the path to peace of mind, I have witnessed his unbelievable offering to the world, his steadfast determination to live the principles he offers. In earlier days, I watched from behind the scenes as he labored with setbacks, unhelpful beliefs or challenges, and never did he give up or fail to change his mind. I carefully watched his inner process, and learned, admired, and emulated his ways. It didn't matter if he didn't know how to do something, he just proceeded anyway with great faith. He was willing to go where others feared to tread, willing to be criticized or condemned for taking actions of love and inclusion and seeing all as equals. He remains courageously at the forefront of demonstrating his deep conviction that everyone is lovable and deserving, and that no matter what, one can always choose peace!

"Completely in character and true to form, Jerry has found yet another way to be helpful to us all, revealing his own private inner processes in this newly discovered collection of early notes and poetry. Through writing of his painful, but ultimately successful path to peace of mind, Jerry once again offers assurance and the promise of a happier life to those for whom life seems less than satisfactory.

"No words can express my gratitude for all I have learned and enjoyed with this 'loving force to be reckoned with,' and I'm sure the millions he has inspired would agree. So take Jerry's hand as he walks, in remembrance, through his own healing and you will find yours as well. He will be right there for you, unfailingly, as he has been for all of us who love him dearly."

— Carol Howe, author of *Never Forget To Laugh:*
Personal Recollections of Bill Thetford,
Co-Scribe of 'A Course In Miracles'
www.carolhowe.com

POETRY AND NOTES TO MYSELF

Poetry and Notes to Myself

My Ups and Downs with
A Course in Miracles

୫ବ

Gerald G. Jampolsky, M.D.

MINI COURSE PUBLISHING
SAUSALITO, CALIFORNIA

Editor: Karen Cirincione, Ph.D.

Cover design: Mariah Parker
www.mettagraphics.com

MINI COURSE PUBLISHING
www.minicoursepublishing.com
3001 Bridgeway, Suite K-368
Sausalito, California 94965
877-244-3392 x705

DEDICATION

I dedicate this book to my soul mate, Diane Cirincione-Jampolsky, Ph.D. When we met in 1981, she came into my life as an angel, teaching me kindness, compassion and tenderness. As spiritual partners, we committed daily to making *A Course in Miracles* a way of finding our way Home. She joined me in committing our lives to experiencing the Oneness of God and making our relationship a Holy Relationship, where we strive to experience the power of Love as our reality.

Our lives have continued to evolve over the last four decades. During this time, we have traveled and worked together, sharing Attitudinal Healing in over 60 countries. We have met many challenges along the way, and Diane continues to nourish me and so many others with her wisdom and unconditional love.

Whatever is beyond love and gratitude, I give to you, Diane, for making our life together and this book such a sacred event.

ACKNOWLEDGMENTS

I want to acknowledge Karen Cir ncione, Ph.D., my sister-in-law, who is a retire l college professor in the field of education. There are no words to adequately express my appreciation for all of Karen's patience, contributions, and help in editing this book. She put her heart and soul and love of poetry and the written wor l into every aspect of this writing.

While working together, Karen ar d I have each found unexpected healing for oursel es in the content of these pages. Perhaps the greatest t enefit we have found in working together is the dee ening of our friendship and the respect and love for one another.

Thank you, Karen. I will be forever grateful.

I would also like to acknowledge with love and deep gratitude Helen Schucman, Bill Thetford, Kenneth Wapnick, Judith Skutch Whitson, Bill Whitson, Bob Skutch, Tamara Morgan, Robert Rosenthal, Marianne Williamson, Carol Howe, Lee Jampolsky, Eulalia and Jack Luckett, Hugh and Gayle Prather, Jeff Seibert, Roger Walsh, Frances Vaughan, Beverly Hutchinson McNeff, Darin and Maria Zakich, and all the staff at Miracle Distribution Center.

You have each touched my spiritual journey in unique and profound ways.

CONTENTS

FOREWORD

I have had the felicity of witnessing the spiritual path of Dr. Gerald Jampolsky. This volume, *Poetry and Notes to Myself*, reflects the early history of Jerry's sometimes tortured path to Self-realization. I had seen some of these writings in late 1978. This is my story of how it happened.

In September, 1973, I was on my way to a Parapsychology Conference in Virginia. I was then living in New York City and teaching courses in Parapsychology and New Dimensions of Healing at New York University. While waiting to change planes in Washington, DC, I met two friends who were going to present their scientific findings about their work with the psychic Uri Geller. A paunchy, grey-haired man in a rumpled seersucker suit wove his unsteady way towards us. He was clearly intoxicated. My friends introduced the Californian as psychiatrist, Dr. Gerald Jampolsky, who was aware of their work. The two scientists quickly moved on to board our connecting flight, and Jerry and I followed them, beginning a conversation about our mutual interest in consciousness research.

That conversation continued throughout the three days of meetings. During that time, it felt to me as if I was reconnecting with a very familiar soul. Indeed, Jerry revealed the complete story of his life from birth until present in such surprisingly rich detail that I remember an inner whisper, "He is catching up since your last lifetime together." He spared nothing even that he felt insignificant, alienated and alone. He admitted he was an alcoholic.

Why do two people, seemingly from different backgrounds, professions and lifestyles, meet with such deep recognition in an airport? Why do their lives interconnect at this juncture with such unknown power to produce a partnership that seemed a necessary part of a Higher Plan?

After that conference, Jerry followed me to my home in New York City to meet my husband, Bob Skutch, and a circle of our like-minded friends. Jerry's keen interest and experiences in his own

life and his practice with children who thought
beyond conventional boundaries echoed my own.
My daughter, Tam, had been born acutely sensitive
to forces that took her past her five senses into a
realm of what some called "The Sixth Sense." Jerry
knew she was being quietly investigated at the
Maimonides Hospital, Brooklyn, New York at the
research facility known as "The Dream Lab."

That seemed enough upon which to base a close
connection. But ours went much further than that.
It quickly got confused with romance and produced
an intensity that brought about guilt and shame. It
flourished with feelings that often included suffering
and confusion. It deteriorated into bursts of rage,
anger and blame. Yet at the core there was always love
and a bond that would not be broken

On May 29, 1975 at Columbia University, School
of Physicians and Surgeons, I met with Drs. Helen
Schucman, William Thetford and Kenneth Wapnick,
who were working in a large office suite together.
The Department of Psychology was their base as
Helen and Bill fulfilled their roles as professors and
researchers. At a memorable lunch, we started to
explore some ideas of unconventional healing, and I
suddenly addressed Helen, blurting out, "Oh, you're
hearing an Inner Voice, aren't you?" I think I was

as shocked as she was. But the door was opened to further discussion in their private office, where they revealed to me their secret history of scribing a manuscript called, *A Course in Miracles*.

I was given a copy of that 1500 page manuscript, held in seven black thesis binders. I immediately called Jerry in Tiburon, California to read him some powerful passages I had already discovered. Never one to waste time, Jerry asked me if I could bring it with me as soon as possible when I next visited the West Coast. I was making many trips to northern California as I was serving on the founding Board of Directors of the new Institute for Noetic Sciences. Ten days later, we were exploring this Course together when Jerry had a remarkable epiphany. He felt as if he had waited for this teaching all his life. He insisted upon speaking with the two scribes immediately to ask them if he could have a copy of this astounding document. After a long introductory personal telephone chat, Helen and Bill agreed.

That was the beginning of a profound change in our relationship. Jerry and I would connect on the phone daily, so I could read the Text to him before we discussed it. We continued through the Workbook, trying to put the theory into practice. We understood for the first time the meaning of a Special

Relationship. We were a perfect illustration of that love/hate syndrome. At times, there were enormous attacks of our egos when Jerry would suggest we stop and intone a Course prayer for those moments:

I give you to the Holy Spirit as part of myself.
I know that you will be released, unless I want to use
you to imprison myself.
In the name of my freedom I choose your release,
because I recognize that we will be released together."
                                                    T- 5.X1.10

Sometimes it worked, sometimes it didn't. We just kept on trying, again and again. Helen and Bill were our personal therapists. They gleaned that through us, two people who were committed to seeing each other in a different and better way, this would be their first opportunity to see the Course in action. We were blessed in having the guidance of the scribes, along with that of our Inner Teacher. With our promise to each other and the Course, we accomplished what we had once thought impossible!

Neither Helen nor Bill lived to see the completion of their work with Jerry and with me. But we know, in Spirit, they are aware and must feel a happy connection in mutuality. To both of us Helen was a strong and stern advisor. She looked upon Jerry as an unfinished work. Sometimes she could be harsh. For his birthday in 1978, she reflected her views of the way she saw him in spirit. She recognized his potential in this poem dedicated to him:

Brother Swan

Let us forget the dark and hurtful ways
We travelled on with you; the twisted feet
That walked against the holy will of God,
Away from peace and from the quiet lake
That was the resting place that he ordained.
The fumbling, failing creature has become
The gift of God. In holy thankfulness
We see in you what each of us can be
And will become with you. You chose for us,
And turned your bleeding feet the other way,
And we give thanks to you who chose for us.
So let us look with wonder upon the swan,
The gift of God, the holy light of Christ,
Resplendent in his shining sinlessness.

The purity of Heaven is your gift
Let us receive it now in thankfulness,
For your release. Your free, unfettered wings
Remind us that your freedom is our own,
Remind us that our freedom is of God.

From "The Gifts of God" by Helen Schucman
Written for Jerry Jampolsky, requested by Judith Skutch Whitson

Jerry responded by having a lovely enamel
pendant designed for her with the image of a swan
on a blue background. For the rest of her life, she
often wore it around her neck as a symbol of her
deep love for him.

Over the years, we saw more and more evidence
of a meaningful change. We dropped our judgments
of each other. We began to see each other through
gentleness. Gratitude became the framework in which
we reflected each other's holiness.

All through this learning process, Jerry was
devoting himself to Spirit more and more. He began
writing inspired poetry and messages to himself. He
gave up alcohol, and he avoided coffee as a stimulant.
His physical appearance reflected this change. He

founded The Center for Attitudinal Healing which, originating in his home town of Tiburon, spread rapidly throughout the world as evidence of the adage: An idea whose time has come.

My husband, Bob, and I separated in form but not in function. We both remarried but remain to this day fulfilling our assignment as founders and directors of the Foundation for Inner Peace, the appointed publisher of the Course. I married Dr. William Whitson, a West Pointer who had spent many years of service in China. At the time we met, he was at the Library of Congress as Chief of Foreign Affairs and National Defense. Within a short time, he joined us as Vice President of the Foundation for Inner Peace, responsible for the Translation Program with Dr. Kenneth Wapnick.

Jerry was then ready for the other great gift of his lifetime. He met Diane Cirincione, truly a soulmate, and they forged a precious life together which continues to bless so many through their offering of deep spiritual counseling and Attitudinal Healing.

I believe this latest publication from Jerry movingly describes his passage from fear to love. Our Special Relationship, healed long ago, is based upon this physician's advice: "to forgive is the prescription for happiness."

Sometimes I am asked if I know of anyone who is actually manifesting the practice taught in *A Course in Miracles*. There are some, but I always cite as my superhero, Jerry Jampolsky. Over the past forty-four years, I have had the unique privilege of experiencing his success in accomplishing an amazing inner shift. I know of no one who has tried harder. He serves as an example to us all.

Judith Skutch Whitson, 2017

Founder and Chair of the Board of Directors
Foundation for Inner Peace
Publisher of *A Course in Miracles* since 1975
www.acim.org

INTRODUCTION

I was an atheist for almost half of my life. My disbelief in God first began when I didn't heed my parents' dire threat that God would strike me dead if I ate bacon.

When I was eight years old and on my first Cub Scout outing, everyone began eating their breakfast of bacon and eggs. The bacon smelled so good that I suddenly decided to eat it. I distinctly remember quickly looking behind me to see if God was there, waiting to strike me dead. Nothing happened, but I continued to feel guilty for a long time afterward. I was scared that my parents' warning would come true because I believed God to be frightening and vengeful. I also adopted my parents' perception that the purpose of life was to suffer and survive in a fearful world where every day someone could threaten or attack you.

When I was sixteen, and a good friend of mine was killed in an automobile accident, I lost the little faith in God I had. I couldn't believe that God would let such a cruel thing happen. And this left me feeling more fearful, vulnerable, and unlovable. Therefore, although part of me rejected God, another part of my mind felt that God was punishing me for all my misdeeds.

When I flunked kindergarten, I was completely devastated. The embarrassment, pain, and the feeling of not being good enough became a common theme throughout my early life. My ego voice gave me a continuous reminder of how stupid I was. I remained in the bottom of my classes in public school and barely got into college. It wasn't until medical school that I discovered I had the learning disability, dyslexia. I struggled through Stanford Medical School and graduated on probation. During my internship, however, I was surprised to learn that one of my professors thought I was the best intern in surgery, and his belief in me gave me some hope that through my education, I would amount to something.

By 1975, the outside world saw me as a successful psychiatrist who appeared to have everything he wanted. But my inner world was chaotic, empty, unhappy, and hypocritical. My twenty-year marriage had recently ended a few

years before in a painful divorce. I had become
an alcoholic and had developed chronic, disabling
back pain as a means of handling guilt. At this
time, my closest relationship was with Judy Skutch
(Whitson). She had just received the unpublished
manuscript of *A Course in Miracles* bringing it
directly to me and telling me it was about God and
spiritual transformation. As a militant atheist, I was
strongly resistant to these topics, but she succeeded
in convincing me to read one page, saying that she
believed that this Course had the power to heal our
"special relationship."

What followed was an experience I have never
been able to fully articulate in words. After reading
that single page, I began to cry. Deep inside me a
tiny voice said, "Physician, heal thyself. This is your
way home." Then I felt the Presence of God and
came to know that my purpose in life was going to
be one of service to others, doing my best to share
love and forgiveness with everyone I met, regardless
of their behavior. This was the beginning of my
spiritual journey.

I began by reading *A Course in Miracles*
Workbook, but the daily lessons were often hard
for me to understand, so eventually Judy and I did
the lessons together, which lasted for several years.

Our relationship began to transform from a "special relationship" to a "Holy Relationship."

Gradually, I began to see that I didn't have to listen to my ego voice, which supported fear and separation. Instead, I could choose to listen to the Voice of God, a Voice based on love and joining. It really didn't take much, though, for me to be attracted to guilt and suffering. In the flash of a second, I would judge the motives and behavior of people around me and suddenly become filled with doubt, distrust, fear, anger, and conflict. I found that I could hear my inner teacher and feel peaceful when I stilled my mind, let go of my guilty past, and came to God with empty hands. I learned that I could choose the thoughts that I put in my mind.

During my spiritual journey, sometimes I found it difficult to distinguish between the voice of my ego and the Voice of God. I had my ups and downs studying the lessons in the Course. At times, I would awaken in the middle of the night and words would pour from me which reminded me of the beauty, joy, peace, and safety that we can all experience by accepting God's Unconditional Love. At other times, I awakened to the terror and cries of my ego, and words from my insane mental state flowed from me. I wrote my thoughts in my journals as diary entries and as poems. At first, I kept these poems private,

using them only to increase my own awareness.
When I began sharing a few of them in my lectures,
I found that others, people who were struggling
through their own dark nights of the soul, felt and
experienced the very same things I was describing.

It was later in 1975 that I, along with others, was
inspired to begin a small center where the principles
from the Course could benefit children and adults
facing life-threatening challenges. I was guided
to choose twelve of the key principles and present
them in a generic way so that peoples of all cultures
and faiths, and even those who were agnostics
or atheists, could all benefit from them. Judy and
I meditated together to see if our Higher Power
could give us a name for the new center. Judy came
up with the name, Center for Attitudinal Healing.
This was the beginning of the first Center offering
free, support services. Now in the fifth decade,
independent Centers and Groups continue to emerge
all around the world.

During the summer of 2016, when my wife,
Diane, was cleaning out our storage area, she found
my journals from decades past. When I listened to
them once again, I was moved, remembering my
own struggles, and thinking that perhaps they could
be helpful to others. I therefore decided to include
many of them in this present book.

I have organized my poems, letters, and notes to myself as well as some from other people and from *A Course in Miracles* into the stages of my spiritual journey: "My Prison of Darkness," "Into the Light," and "Love is the Answer." I have also included a section of "Spiritual Reminders," which in one or two sentences provide the essence of a truth I learned during my journey with *A Course in Miracles*.

Additionally, because forgiving ourselves as well as others is essential to attaining inner peace, I have also included in the Author's Note, "Forgiveness, The Greatest Healer of All," a poem I wrote which includes the great peace one can attain through forgiveness.

I was fifty years old when I consciously started my spiritual journey, and now, at ninety-two, I am still a student of *A Course in Miracles*. Every morning, Diane and I read a lesson from the *Course*, meditate on it, discuss it, and do our best to remember it throughout the day. While God's Light has become more consistent in our lives, we find that retraining our minds takes a continual commitment.

My hope is that you may find some inspiration and peace of mind within these pages and with your own spiritual journey.

Gerald G. Jampolsky, M.D.

Part One

MY PRISON OF DARKNESS

Help Me Out of My Prison of Darkness

Help me out of my prison of darkness
    created by the shadows of my ego.

Awaken me from my dream of fear
    where guilt, blame, and attack beckon
    from shadowed doors.

Help me to see the world differently
    by finding no value in blame
    and self-condemnation.

Help me to experience Love
    as my only reality.

Help me to cross only
    the bridges of forgiveness
    that I may come out of darkness
    into the Light.

Guilt

Guilt, you are my false security blanket
    that assures me of continual
    suffering.
You are the nemesis of my being.

You are my judge, jailer and jail
    all wrapped into one.
You keep me immobilized in a
    continual state of self bondage
    and self punishment.

You put me in jail and throw away
    the key.
You keep me in darkness, alone and
    in a state where there is no love
    and no hope.

You make me lose all faith and trust.
You hold in me a state where there is
    only self hate and projected hate,
    where I hate God, the world and
    everyone in it.
You are my certain prescription for
    insanity.

continues

You make sure that every time I try to
   rid myself of you, my blanket of guilt,
   by kicking you off of me, I grab you
   and cling to you with all my might.
You have convinced me that I cannot
   live without you.

I Have Felt Lost Most of My Life

I have felt lost most of my life, and it is only
   today that I equate losing my way and
   feeling empty inside as one and the same.

When I have chosen to let my heart shrink and
   be empty of love, I manufacture that state of
   loneliness and separation that has plagued me
   most of my life.

When will I awaken to know, without any
   doubts whatsoever, that I have been
   looking for my identity in the external world?
   I have been looking in the wrong place.

Help me only to look inside so that I may be
   home once again, so that I can stop this endless
   wandering in a circle that goes nowhere.

Fear

Fear, what lightning speed you have!

With the blink of an eye, you fill my
    heart and mind with terror.

You make my heart pound with
    apprehension of my own
    destruction.
You produce a state of separation,
    isolation and aloneness that
    is beyond despair.

Fear, my nightmare of deception,
    you tried to convince me that Love
    has vanished from my being,
    never to return again.

Creative Love Force of the Universe,
    I hold my arms out to you
    and pray for your help.

Awaken me and transform my fear
into my true state of Love.
Awaken me to the truth that there is
no fear, that there is only Love.
Awaken me to the truth that there is
no separation and that we are
joined in Love as One forever.

I Know I'm Not Rejected

I know I'm not rejected, but I feel rejected.

I know that God doesn't reject me.

I want to feel God's Love all the time and to
identify only with the Spirit Selves in others
rather than their behavior.

I will never feel God's Presence if I am concerned
with form of any kind and make my love
conditional on what that form should be.

Obstacles to Peace

What is this cancer inside me,
    the fiery anger that lingers
    in its thin disguise,
    the coldness and the brittleness
    that comes from my pores
    at a moment's notice?

Could it all be fear,
    and nothing but fear?
Is there no roadmap
    that can lead me to peace
    and freedom?

Can I really feel
    whole and at one
    by simply crossing
    the bridge of forgiveness?

Why does something
    that seems so simple
    bring out my greatest
    resistance?

continues

Obstacles, obstacles, obstacles
is that all there is to life,
a series of obstacles
separating me from others?

When will I awaken to
the full awareness that all obstacles
between myself and others
are self-imposed?

I have manufactured them
through my own fear of love
and my own fear of God.

The House of Fear

Let me awaken from this world of darkness,
  from this house of fear that I have built.

Let me arise from this dream world I have made,
  a fear house of mirrors, of terror that has
  no end in sight.

Let me be released from the prison I have made,
  a dream world filled with illusions of fear that
  never disappear.

Let me escape from the revolving door of
  frustration that I seem to be trapped in.

Let me ascend into Your Arms and Heart
  that I have never truly left.

Let the Rip Van Winkle in me disappear.

Let Your Light shine away all the dark shadows
  that have kept me asleep.

continues

Let me be born anew with the Light of Christ
    shining in me and return to the House of Love
    that You created and from where I never really left.

Let my long, misguided journey be over.

Let me be home at last in Your Heart of Love,
    the House of Love of Your Creation, never
    to feel lost or separated from You ever again.

Bitter Agony

Oh, what bitter agony.
How hellish is the dark night of my soul.
How seemingly impossible are my feelings of
unrest.
How my heart feels like it has shrunk into oblivion.

When will I learn that longing for anything
or anyone
on this planet earth
can only bring me pain,
can only make me feel alone,
rejected, and unlovable?

When will I learn?
When will I learn?

When will I learn that I'm never alone when I am
experiencing Oneness with my Loving Creator?

Help Me Awaken From the
World of Opposites

Help me awaken from the
   world of opposites
   where I seem to dream of
   terror, pain and isolation.

Let the passing of this dream be my
   awakening to reality.

Help me see Love as everlasting and
   all encompassing and
   having no opposites.

Let me remember that bodies are not real.

Give me the strength to see physical death
   as only an illusion, and let me
   identify only with Joy and Love
   which are ever present.

Letting Go

Help me to let go of my preoccupation
    with the future.
Give me the strength to stop
    my futile attempts
    to predict and control the future.
Let me see no value in my plan
    of what the future should be.

Rid me of my senseless questions
    about tomorrow and of
    all my desires to manipulate
    and control others so that the
    future can be to my making.

Remind me that my fears and uncertainties
    of tomorrow are only related to
    my unfounded fear of You.

Help me to be still and
    help me to listen and love.

Awaken me to the truth of Your Presence,
    being only in the now of this moment.

continues

Lift me up into Your Arms and remind me
  that I am Your Creation,
  and that I am the Perfection of Love.

Help me to acknowledge that I am
  Your Messenger of Love,
  and free me to shine
  Your Light everywhere.

Let me feel Your Freedom within me, and
  let me laugh at the illusions
  that my ego once made me
  feel were so real.

Let me be light. Let me be joy. Let me know
  that I am the reflection of You
  wherever I am and wherever I go.

Let me let go.
Let me let God.
Let me lighten up.

Let Me See Love Within an I Without

Oh God, I want so much to join You,
    not tomorrow, but now.
And yet, the external world seems so real,
    so attacking. I feel so alone.

How can I feel You within when I feel
    guilty, rejected, unloved?
I know it is a cloud of illusion, but oh,
    it feels so real.

Please take my guilt away.
Please take my anger away.

Let my heart sing perfect forgiveness.
Let my heart dance to the music
    without guilt, without pain and only Love.

Let not my ears and eyes deviate from
    Your Healing Heart.
Let me always look within to find You
    before I look outside of my heart.
Let me see Love within and without
    for there is nothing else real to see.

Money, Money, Money

Money, money, money, what a cunning teacher
   you have been.
You have been the pot of gold at the end
   of the rainbow that promised me
   lasting happiness.

What an illusive goal you have been!
What a slippery fish you have been!
I have made you a heart maker,
   yet you have become a heart breaker.
I have given you love, thinking you were love.

Money, money, money, I thought you were my
   measurement of success, my yardstick
   of life and love.
I've let you be my master that has controlled and
   put me in distress, yet I have used you as
   a whip in life.
You have been a fearful god and a loving god
   all wrapped into one.

You have been a means and an end.
I thought you were what I wanted.

I have camouflaged you in fear.
You made the external world real to me.
You have been a filter for my eyes and ears.

I have used you as a sleeping pill.
I've let you make me ill.
You have never made me full at all
You have never let me see the treasure of love
    inside me.

Money, money, money, you have been a teacher of
    emptiness to me.
You have been a god of getting and holding on and
    never getting enough.

Every time I have made you a god of my security,
    my god of the future, I have become dead inside.
How could you have looked like light,
    yet be filled with darkness?
How tricky my perception can be.
How upside down my perception can be.
How attached I have been to you.
How angry you have made me.
How I blamed you for everything.

continues

25

And oh, how I have loved you!
Money, money, money, I thank you for your lessons.
I thank you for teaching me what is real.
You have taught me that money will never buy me
spiritual fulfillment within.
I have learned that if I make money a god, I cut
myself off from love.
If I make giving love a goal, I awaken to
God's Peace.

I used to think that having and holding made
my reality.
I now believe that the Love that created me
is formless,
and it is only the content of my spiritual reality
that leads me to live a life that is based on love.

Now I enjoy experiencing my Oneness with God.
Money is no longer a god for me when I
remind myself that I am the light of the world
and so is everyone else
regardless of their behavior.

The Oneness of You

The Oneness of You is all I desire.
Help me to stop the static of the myriad
    thoughts that cross my mind.
Help me to quiet my mind that I may
    hear Your Voice.

Let me see Light in place of bodies,
    so that I may experience unity
    instead of separation.

Let me hear only the Music of Your Love
    being extended through me.

Let me seek only to give and forgive that
    I may remember I am whole and that
    You are my Source.

Control, Control, Control

Control, control, control, you are the battery,
    the driving force of my ego.

Every time I have tried to control and to predict,
    I've ended up with my plan and with conflict,
    and I have given priority to the identification
    of a body to hurt me.

Every time I have created an expectation for
    another person's behavior based on my ego needs,
    I've ended up in pain and conflict,
    and I've interfered with the other person's freedom
    and my own.

Freedom means not being of the body; it is being
    of Spirit, being of God.

Freedom means releasing others and ourselves
    from the limitations of the body
    and the separation from God.

Freedom means having absolutely no expectation
    for anyone's behavior.

Freedom means to live and move in God.

Every time we interpret another person's behavior,
 we make the body real.

Every time we judge another person's behavior to
 determine their guilt or innocence,
 we make the body real.

Every time we dwell in and are attached to past hurts,
 we make the body real.

To be as God created us, we need to:
 not interpret,
 not judge and
 not live in the past.

The External World

Oh external world how deceptive you are,
    changing, changing, changing,
    all the while tempting and luring me
    to find peace and happiness.

When will I learn not to make your treason
    my goal?
When will I learn that the external world
    does not cause my happiness
    or sadness?

Oh dear God, help me to know that my happiness and
    peace have nothing to do with what is external but
    only to what is internal.

Help me go inside and find your quietness there.
Help me go inside so I can feel united with you.
Help me to know that I have no needs that are not
    being fully met by You right now.

Help me to know that when I go inside,
    I find You in my heart,
    filling my mind with Your Thoughts.
Help remind me that when I go inside before I look
    without, I will feel love, peace, and unity.

Letting Go of Fear

What is this heaviness I have felt
    on my journey through life?

What is this constant feeling of
    limitation and restriction?

What brings on this heaviness in my chest,
    constriction in my breathing,
    and the imprisonment of my soul?

The weight on my shoulders and the
    chain and balls of steel around
    my ankles are always the same -
    fear and guilt.

If I truly want to be free,
    if I truly want to be let out of
    my self-imposed imprisonment,
    I must retrain my mind
    and learn to let go of all the fear
    and guilt I have so diligently held on to.

I must learn to see absolutely no value
    in either fear or guilt,
    only then will I be free
    of limitations and restrictions,
    only then will my imprisoned spirit
    of love be released.

I Am Tired of the Journey of Seeking

I am tired of the journey of seeking
that leads to emptiness.

I am tired of running in a circle,
only to find myself again in pain.

Help me to leave this world of illusion
and find myself in You.

Jerry, If You Want to Be Depressed

Jerry, if you want to be depressed,
heavy and morose,
hang on to that guilt with all your might.

But if you want to be happy, light, and at peace,
let go of your guilt
with all your might.

Desire

Oh desire, what a tumultuous pathway
    we have traveled together.
One moment you seem like a friend, indeed,
    leading me to where the treasures of the
    world have remained hidden from me.

Oh, what a deceptive friend you have been;
    what a disappointment you have been.
Every treasure I have sought in this world
    through your interference has sooner or later
    brought me sadness, emptiness, and conflict.
Oh what a fiery dance of ego you are.

To me you seem insatiable and never satisfied.
You are the god of inconsistency and illusions.
Every time I've let you become the horse and the
    rein of my mind, every goal that I thought would
    bring me happiness has become a mirage.

Seek but do not find has been your motto.
You have betrayed me, and I've allowed you to
    lead me to become a victim of my senses.

You have always promised me everlasting
    happiness, but what have I found?
I have found a merry go round of torture and
    sacrifice, a circle of hell where every pleasure
    sooner or later becomes pain.

You are a god of greed, a god of me-ism, a god
    of get-ism, a god of separation, a god of the body
    that promises me that the desires of this body will
    bring me happiness untold.

But what have I found? I have found that you have
    never brought me satisfaction for long.
You have tempted me to be attached to the past
    and to the future, but then I see this is not
    what I want; I want something that is spiritually
    fulfilling.

What a master of trickery you are.
You have taught me that it is always greener
    on the other side of the hill.
You have been a master teacher of having me
    think of myself first, to be greedy, and to hold
    on to things.

                     continues

You have promised me unlimited satisfaction.
You have encouraged me to become king of the
    world, ruler of the universe.
You have led me to believe that the world is mine
    to mold, and yet every time I think I have molded
    the world I want, the world shifts.

Oh desire, what a double personality you are and
    how you talk with two tongues.
You promise me satisfaction and salvation, and
    yet you leave me never consistently satiated,
    satisfied or peaceful.

Oh desire, you have promised me reality and yet
    everything I've valued on the earth
    has turned out to be an empty illusion.

Oh desire, what a master of ambiguity and
    ambivalence you are.
How still and peaceful I can be and then within
    an instant, you become the heartbeat of my ego.
You become an earthquake and a tornado all in one,
    and I feel destroyed, empty, and longing to
    experience love.

Oh desire, where have I gone wrong that I have
    allowed myself to be your victim?

Oh when will I learn the lesson that the desire of
    what my senses seem to want will always keep
    me as your victim?

Oh God, dear Father, please help me out of this
    illusionary world.
Help me find eternal peace.

Dear innocent child, you have forgotten what you are.
You have fallen asleep and forgotten that peace and
    happiness eternal are always yours.
You have forgotten that you are the essence of love, you
    are peace, you are joy.
I created you as Love, you are always part of Me, and
    you will always have My Total Love.
There is no separation, there is no time, no space.
You have no needs.
You are love and love has no needs, no desires,
    no strivings.
Love is the only thing there is.
Love is everything there is.

continues

Wake up my child.
Have no desires of the world you see
    for the world you see with your physical eyes
    is but an illusion and valueless.

Wake up my child and have but one desire--
    the desire to truly only want to experience the
    Peace of God.
Desire only the reality of love that is invisible to
    the eye.
Know that your reality is Spirit, not body.
Spirit has no desire.
Only the illusionary body has desires.

Dear child of God, have faith in me, see only the
    Light in the world and know that you are the
    Light of the world.

Oh child of God, have but one desire.
Have only the desire to experience My Love and
My Peace which are eternal and are always
    there for you.

Pain

Pain is ego's last ditch stand that attempts to deny
the existence of Our Creator.

Pain calls attention to the body and represents the
ego's energy at making the body seem real.

Fear and guilt form the foundation for pain which
results in feelings of separateness.

Pain, therefore, is a defense against the realization of
Our Creator and the experience of AT-ONE-MENT.

Part Two

INTO THE LIGHT

When I Was a Little Boy

When I was a little boy, I became lost
in a department store
at Christmas time.
Panic, fear, and the thought I was abandoned is what
I remember most.

The fear of abandonment has been
a recurrent theme
in my life.

It has taken me all these years to realize that my
basic fear
was that God had abandoned me.

What a feeling of freedom it is to know at last that
God has never abandoned me
and never will.

Let Us Take Each Other's Hands

Let us take each other's hands
  and walk toward the Light of God.
Let us stay in the Presence of God
  and in the Nowness of Joy.

Let us be free from separation
  of all kinds.
Let us resist the temptation
  to judge each other's behavior.

Let us stop our suffering.
Let us, together, once and for all,
  let go of our past hurts
  and unmet desires.

Let us put our total trust in God and
  then see only the God-Self in each other
  and feel God's Never-ending Love
  filling us to the brim and over.

Let us let go of all our self-doubts
  that we have projected on to each other.

continues

45

Let us join our wills as one
 and be directed only by God's Plan.

Let us join in Love.
Let us join in Joy.
Let us join in Peace.
Let us Love, Love, Love.

Beyond Suffering

Remind me that when I am in the Heart of God,
    there is no suffering. There is no pain.

Help me to be compassionate and
    identify with the dignity of Love
    in all whom my eyes would behold.

Remind me that the gift of peace and
    unconditional love
    is the most valuable thing
    I can give to anyone.

Let me look past the pain that
    human suffering would tempt me
    to identify with and to see only
    the Light of Love enveloping and
    emanating from all living forms.

Help me to know that Your Love
    is my only reality and to know
    that what is true and real
    can never be hurt or harmed.

continues

Let me be the beacon of Your Light that
heals all pain, suffering, and separation.

Let me feel the beating of Your Heart
within me, that I may shine
Your Love and Light on all
and know that the Light I see
is but a reflection of Your Light
and my Light joined as One.

Remind me to be grateful for Your Love
and for the opportunity to be
helpful and loving to all others.

Another Way of Looking at "Getting"

Help us not to exclude anyone, and teach us the way
   to extend our unlimited love unconditionally.

Let us recognize that fear is the result of our
   preoccupation with what we want to get, or what we
   think we are not getting, or trying to evaluate why we
   don't get what we want.

And help us to recognize that the more we analyze and
   focus on the getting and the not getting, the more
   fear we will have.

Help us to accept that the solution does not come from
   further intellectual analysis.

But let us accept the knowledge that the solution comes
   the instant we make the decision to view everyone
   and everything with the eyes and ears of Our Creator.

Everything is Forgivable

Everything is forgivable.

When we truly realize that
nursing a grievance is injurious
to our health and happiness, we can let go.

Forgiveness doesn't mean that we condone
or agree with what happened.

It simply means that we're
willing to heal our own minds
by no longer seeing any value
in holding on to anger.

The Cry of Children

The cry of children still rings in my ears.
I have just come from the dispensary unit
    at a Sudanese Refugee Camp, located near
    the border of Ethiopia.

Their cries were of hunger and pain. Their
    cries to me were for peace, love, and
    tranquility.

Their cries were appeals for sanity and help
    in a world that is filled with the dichotomies
    of the haves and have nots.

To me, their cries were cries of the soul
    that first broke my heart and then opened it up
    to truly wanting to live a selfless life that is
    directed at only helping and loving others.

Let us give and give, and still give more
    until we have given all of ourselves and
    all of our love to those who are
    suffering and in pain.

God's Love is Never in a Hurry

Go slowly and then be still.
There is no need to run.

You never need to hurry when
    you live in the nowness of this moment.

Just remember
God's Love is never in a hurry;
    it is only in the present
    when we let go of the past and future.

When you know that God's Love is
    always with you, there is never anything
    to run away from or anything to run to.

Just remember
Be still and experience
    the eternal Peace of God.

Disappointment

We will be disappointed sooner or later if it is
our own plan that we hold dear to our heart
rather than God's plan.

Disappointment comes when our happiness
depends on getting what we want and
on our attachment to it.

Disappointment is always an ego function
and is never a function of God.

God's Will for us is perfect happiness right now.
God's Will for us is to have our will and
His Will as one, to join and extend His Love
now, in the everlasting, ever-present now.

Let us let go of our own personal plan for the future.
Let us let go of our attachment to the disappointment
of the past.
Let us acknowledge God's Love.

continues

Father, I am so grateful for the completion and totality
  of Your Love for me.
My only desire is to be the bearer of Your Gifts.
My joy is to carry out Your Will for me now.
My peace comes from experiencing my gratefulness
  for our joining now and forevermore.

When I Am Feeling Weary

When I am feeling weary and under strain,
    when my body feels as if it's been beaten
    for endless hours, when my stomach feels
    like it is in a knot, I am seeing value in
    holding on to guilt and self-attack.

I find it helpful to forgive myself and the world
    and take this moment as a brand new moment,
    detached from the past and the future and to
    see value in wanting Peace of God as my one goal.

When I give my guilt and despair to the teachers
    within me, I see how rapidly I experience love,
    joy and happiness.

When I trust God with all my might, when I give all
    my problems to God to solve,
    I find how effortless
    the sun shines away the morning mist, rainbows
    appear after dark clouds, and love blooms in
    everything I think of, see, or touch.

And wherever I am, I experience God's Love,
    your love, and my love—all as one.

Hold My Hand

Hold My Hand and become One with Me.

Feel My Presence within at all times.

Let My Presence light up only the present and dissolve all doubts of darkness of the past and future.

And then feel the blissful peace and experience the grace that comes from the fulfillment of My Guidance.

Patience

The impatient are always
    in a hurry.
They are trapped in the future
    attached to fear and time.
The impatient follow self-made
    goals that go nowhere.

The patient are never
    in a hurry.
They are totally in the present,
    bathed in timeless loving.
The patient have no need for goals,
    except to be Home
    in the Heart of God.

The patient are patient
    because they know
    they are already there.

Forgive

Forgive,
    forgive,
    and forgive some more.

Never stop forgiving,
    for the temptation to project
    and judge will always be there
    as long as you are living in the body.

Forgiveness is the key to peace and happiness
    and gives us everything
    that we could possibly want.

Children of the Universe

Children of the Universe,
our hope for the future lies with you.
May we have the courage of listening to
your voices and the wisdom of your faith
that peace is a choice.

May we also look into your eyes and
experience your innocence and know that
your innocence is really our innocence also.

Let us learn from you the power and the ease
of forgiveness as we let go of our
past hurts and distrusts and begin with
a new presence of peace,
the peace that shines brighter than the sun.

Let us awaken to the truth that peace and
holiness are our natural state.

Love and Let Go

Love and let go.
Hold onto nothing.

Let go of your plan for predicting the future.
Let God's Plan be your plan.
Let God be your only Director.

See, hear and feel the world only through
the Love of God in your heart.

Let go and let God.

When I Trust God with All My Might

When I trust God with all my might,
  when I give all of my problems to God to solve,
  I find how effortlessly the sun shines away the
  morning mist.

Rainbows appear after dark clouds, love blooms in
  everything I think of, see, or touch,
  and wherever I am

I experience God's Love.
I experience your love.
I experience my love – all as one.

Honesty

To be honest is to demonstrate
    a total lack of any deception.
It is to omit nothing
        because of our own fears
        of being attacked or rejected.

To be honest we need to be
        totally free of guilt and fear,
        to recognize that either
        we are honest—or we are not,
        and there is no in-between.

To be honest is to experience the
        perfect harmony of having only
        loving thoughts, loving words,
        and loving deeds.

It is to take full responsibility
        for our own behavior and
        to blame no one for anything.

To be honest is to be perfectly free
        and unafraid to be exactly
        what we are...LOVE.

Our Inner Voice

Our Inner Voice is available to all of us.

It can't be used to meet our ego desires,
and it doesn't provide us with a charmed life.

But it does give us something much more important:
a sense of Divine Connection and Guidance.

State of Denial

Alcoholics like I was can often live
in a state of denial about
their alcoholism.

Part of the suffering experienced
comes from denying the existence of
something greater than ourselves.

The People of the World

Dear God, help me to have hope
    for the people of the world.

Rid me of doubts that hunger and deprivation
    put in my mind.

Help me to let go of the measuring sticks that bind
    the future to the miserable past.

Keep my heart full of Your Love and full of faith
    of what the miracle of Your Love can do.

Let my whole being be filled with Your Spirit
    that I may extend Your Love, Your Peace,
    Your Joy, and Your Hope to all.

The Miracle of the Butterfly

Letting go and forgiveness are one and the same.
Their function is to let emotional attachment and
   investment in the past dissolve.
Their purpose is to let us experience
   Oneness with God.

When applied to "special relationships," letting go
   and forgiveness permit us to free ourselves
   from the imprisonment in someone else, under the
   guise that the other person has something we need.

Letting go and forgiveness are like
   transcending the barriers and limitations of the
   cocoon, to become the essence of joy and freedom
   and beauty that we see in the butterfly.

It is the Oneness we see when
   the color and hues of the butterfly's wings
   blend imperceptibly with a vibrant flower.

It allows us to experience the essence of our own love
   as One with everything in the Universe.

When we let go and forgive
    in a special relationship, we experience
    the miracle of immediately dissolving
    jealously, possessiveness, exclusiveness,
    and the feelings of "missing."

The feeling of wanting to
    get something from another person;
    the need to control, manipulate, and
    predict the behavior of another person,
    simply vanishes.

The love/hate of special relationships,
    hating or loving according to whether
    one's imagined needs are met or not,
    also disappears.

The result of this miracle is that we remember and
    recognize that our only essence is Love,
    and Love needs nothing. Its only function is to
    co-create.

continues

The miracle of the butterfly is symbolically the
transformation of a special relationship into
a Holy One, through letting go of the chains of
our self-imposed imprisonment.

The miracle of the butterfly is the knowledge that
we are One with each other and with God forever.

Entering Our Higher Consciousness

Any time we want to
    hurt another person,
    any time a nation wants to
    hurt another nation,
    we have lost our spiritual core.

When we remember
    we are always one with Our Creator,
    the ego world of excuses to
    hurt or be at war disappears.

We then enter our Higher
    Consciousness where our
    only reality is Love,
    and all thoughts of warring
    disappear.

Traveling in the Fast Lane

When we are traveling in the fast lane in life,
    we are acting as if there is some place that
    is more important to be than where we are.

When we travel the fast lane, the future becomes
    more important than the present, and we may
    become confused about whether we are running
    away from something or running to something.

Running in the fast lane has as its companion fear.
    Without fear, we would be content to be in the
    present and to bathe in its peace which is totally
    devoid of fear.

Let us let go of our old compulsion of what we need
    to do in the future.
    Let us remember that God is always to be found
    in the still, quiet lane of the present.

Let our being unfold in the holiness of this eternal
    moment where our spirit reflects the magnitude
    and the quiet of the purity of the calmest of lakes,
    where everything can be seen and nothing is hidden.

Let each moment of our life be a reflection of the
   gentleness and the peace of love in the stillness of
   this moment, where there is no separation and
   everything and everyone are joined.

You Are Never Alone

Wake up, my child.

When we go beyond this world, there is a state of no
time, where there is no such thing as age.

There is no past or future, only the now.

When there is a state of no time or space,
there is but one ultimate truth:
We are limitless love with no boundaries and no form.

Wake up from your dream.
Take off your masks which are made of fear.
Discard your dreams of a world of comparisons
and opposites.

Wake up, my child, and know your innocence,
your grace, and your bliss.

Wake up, my child, and know there is no separation
and that you are never alone.

Wake up, my child, and know that
you are One with Me.

Timelessness

May we know what is real and what is false.

May we live in a world of timelessness
   where there are
   no clocks or yesterdays and tomorrows.

May we stretch our imagination to the fullest
   and know that
   what is real is timeless.

When I Feel Fearful or Depressed

When I feel fearful or depressed
I remind myself
that my fearful child
has reappeared
feeling it is deprived.

Rather than being upset
as I used to be in the past
I now smile and nourish
that fearful child with love
and presto!

The happy child
with a full heart
awakens within me
and once again
I discover
the innocence
that has always been there.

How Will I Know?

How do I know when I hear Your Voice?
How do I know that my ego is not masquerading
   in a costume to deceive me once again?

You will feel the extension of Our Love in the
   harmony of what you think, say, and do.
You will feel My Perfect Peace and Light unending
   without any limitations.

You will see only value in listening to My Voice,
   the Voice of the Holy Spirit and have the
   single goal of peace of mind, Peace of Creation.
You will experience our only function as forgiveness.

Let Me Learn From Children

Dear God, let me learn from children
the secret of love
and the secret of life.

Let me become the smell of the roses,
and the voices in the
garden of children's laughter.

Let me become the tears of their eyes,
and let me become
their peace as they sleep.

Let me become their shining light that makes
all worries and despair disappear.

Dear God, let me find You and myself in them.

The Loving Boomerang

Do you know what I have?
I have a boomerang
A boomerang, of course, is something
you send out that returns to you.

What I have discovered is that
I am like a boomerang.
And every time I send my loving
boomerang out with love,
it comes back to me with love.

Sometimes I make a mistake and
forget what I am.
I forget that I am only love.
When I forget what I am, I sometimes send
anger and fear out with my boomerang,
and anger and fear come back to me.

In a way, my boomerang is my teacher.
It teaches me that everything I give, I receive.
It teaches me that giving and receiving
are one in the same.

From Fear to Love

Fear separates us from each other
 and from Our Source.

Isn't it time to move away from the endless stream
 of conflicted thoughts and toward the only answer
 that can transform not only our individual thoughts
 but also the world?

Perhaps rather than another ideology, what we need
 is a spiritual transformation that encompasses
 everyone and everything.

For this to happen, we need to turn from fear to love.

Not Giving Our Power Away

The way to suffer in this world is to give
   power to people or conditions to
   decide whether we will be happy or not.

The way to be happy in this world is
   to take complete responsibility
   for what we think, say, and do.

Choose Once Again

May I choose the benefits of learning
    to choose once again

When my very foundation
    seems to have disappeared;

When there seems to be a serious question
    about meeting my basic needs of food and rent;

When my future seems to be in terrible doubt
    and the world seems very unfair;

When my heart feels it is skipping beats,
    and I am having trouble catching my breath;

When it feels that I am in shock and that
    someone has punched me in the stomach;

When it feels that it is no longer safe to trust
    and that there is a temptation for me to blame
    someone else for the predicament I am in;

When I feel fragmented, as if I were a jig saw
    puzzle that has been thrown up into the air,
    feeling that it is impossible to be put
    back together again;

When it feels as if God has lost my file
    and has abandoned me, and that all my
    previous faith and trust was wrongly placed
    and that I will never be able to trust
    or have faith in others or God again;

When I have forgotten that the essence
    of my being is Love;

I can be absolutely sure of one thing –
    it is not that God has abandoned me
    but that I have abandoned God and
    I can choose once again.

Shortcuts to God

A Shortcut to God is…

Letting go of interpreting other people's
    behavior,
Letting go of all our judgments,
Letting go of our control issues,
Letting go of guilt, blame and shame,
Letting go of making others wrong
    and ourselves right,
Letting go of our expectations and
    our scripts for others,
Letting go of our assumptions,
Letting go of seeing the shadows of the past
    in others and in ourselves,
Letting go of all our unforgiving
    and self-condemning thoughts.

A Shortcut to God is…

Having the same interest in others
    as we have in ourselves,
Choosing to have peace of mind,
    and the Peace of God as our only goal,
Having a fire in our hearts
    to surrender to Love,

Knowing that our identity is the essence of Love
    and that we are no longer fearful of death.
Choosing peace instead of conflict,
Choosing to cooperate rather than compete,
Believing that giving is receiving,
Knowing that Love is the answer to every problem
    that we will ever face.

A Shortcut to God is…

Trusting and having faith in a
    loving, non-judgmental God,
Stepping aside and letting our Higher Power
    lead the way,
Knowing that we are always loved by God.

A Shortcut to God is…
Knowing that when we've done all of the above,
    Eternal Peace, Love, Joy and Happiness,
    will be ours.

My Dear Friend, My Still Mind

Oh my beautiful, adorable friend,
    how much I have missed you.
    I searched, and searched, and searched
    and found you nowhere.

And now, today, I found you, once again.
You have been here all of the time.
How foolish I have been.
I have looked for you in the wrong place.

In the busyness of my pursuit,
    I sought you in my external world.
I overlooked that
    you were in my inner world all the time.
I neglected to recognize that
    you are my inner world,
        that you are me.

Oh, my dear friend, my still mind,
    you have been here all the time,
    quiet, but nevertheless here.

Part Three

LOVE IS THE ANSWER

Love is the Answer

Whatever the question, love is the answer.
Whatever the problem, love is the answer.
Whatever the fear, love is the answer.
Whatever the pain, love is the answer.
Love is always the answer because
Love is all there is.

The Gift of Love

What gift is there to give but Love.
What song is there to sing but Love.
What prayer is there to pray but Love.
What light is there to join but Love.

We are the Light of all Love.
We are the mirror of Creation's Love.
We are the Essence of Love.

The Moment of Truth

The moment of truth for me
is when I can experience no separation
between myself and others and creation.

The moment of truth for me
is total surrender to God and
being totally guided by the Voice of God.

The moment of truth for me
is that Love is the only reality.
Words are no longer necessary.

The Glorious Lights Are Shining

The glorious lights are shining.
The angels are singing and dancing.
The air is filled with excitement.
The celebration is about to begin.

The lights are expanding and joining,
and as we feel the eternal oneness
of their luminance, time stops, and
the world disappears.
The truth of our unity with God
is all that remains.

I Am

I am the Will of God.

I am the purity of love, joy, and peace united as one.
I am the essence of giving and of joining.
I am the state of mind where there is total absence
    of fear, guilt, anger and hate, pain and sickness,
    and judgment and separation of any kind.
I am the reflection of God's Love,
    and hence, I am everywhere;
I have no boundaries and no form.

I am the light of the world,
    and hence, I am a reflection of all that is beautiful.
I am a reflection of the simplicity of
    the flowers, the sand on the beach,
    the singing of the birds,
    the sound of the waves on the shore,
    and the stillness of the lake.
I am a reflection of all that
    is gentle, kind, tender, compassionate, and
    of all that is trusting and honest.
I am that state of mind where there is only
    eternal life and there is no death, and
    where there is only happiness.

I am the essence of Spirit,
    and it is my spiritual being that is my identity.
I am whole and united with all life.
I am invisible and immeasurable.
I am God's Holy Child of Love;
I am God's Creation; God is my Cause, and
    I am God's Effect.
I am Co-creator of Love with God.

God's Will and my will are one.
If ever I accept anything else as my will,
    I deny what I am.
I am a reflection of the Will of God.

The Miracle of the Sunrise

I love the early morning before the sun rises.

There is a special hush, stillness and tranquility
that sets the stage for the awakening
to Our Creator's Presence.

The Gifts of God

The gifts of God are:

To know that we are
  always loved completely and totally
To know that we will never be abandoned
To know we will never be alone
To know we are always lovable
To know we are an eternal, spiritual being that is only
  temporarily in a body
To know there is no separation
To know that we are one with Our Source and all
  that is life
To know that loving kindness and happiness are
  our natural state
To know we are here only to be truly helpful
To know that our true reality is Love, and that Love is
  the only thing and everything there is
To know that true Love casts out all fear
To know that we are the innocent child of God
To know that we are the Light of the world and
To know that we are here to teach only Love.

Trust

To be trusting is to know that only the knowledge
of Love is what can be trusted.

It is to recognize that the perception of all that we
see and hear continues to change and can never
be trusted.

To be trusting is to trust in only that which does not
change the eternal.

It is not to build your trust on what personalities or
bodies may or may not do.

To be trusting is to trust in Love, trust in the spiritual
essence of all people.

It is to have total trust and faith with no doubts
whatsoever in Our Creator as your only true
relationship.

Infant Child

Infant child you are my teacher
    with your joy and perfect innocence.

Your oneness with everything about you
    is the mirror of my essence.

Your eternal light and love are
    the mirror of the Universe.

You are my true reflection and
    represent Heaven's Love.

Wherever I Go, You Walk Along with Me

God, hold me in Your Arms.

Help me to know that You are
always inside of me
in the center of my being.

Help me know that wherever I go,
wherever I am,
You walk along with me.

In Gratitude to You

My whole being pulsates
   with the fire of desire
   for our everlasting union.
My very breath is but Yours.
My heart is a limitless beacon
   of Your Love.

My Spirit, being Yours, is the Light of the World.
My eyes but radiate and reflect
   our Perfect Love.
My very essence vibrates with You as the
   harmony of music not yet heard.

My vision is but Your Love
   flowing through me,
   seeing only its own reflection.
My only fulfillment is following Your
   Directions and Guidance.

My voice, being Yours, can only bless.
My prayer is but an eternal song of gratitude,
   that You are in me, and I am in You,
   and that I live in Your Grace forever.

To Be

What is it just to be?

It is to see the Love of God
in yourself and everyone.

It is to have a song of Love in your heart
which brings a smile of happiness to your face.

It is to know that you need do nothing to be loved.

It is to know that you are Love,
you are forever God's Creation
and that God Loves you
totally and forever.

It is to know that in just being God's Love,
through you it is constantly being given away.

I Felt the Power of God's Love

I felt the Light within me today.

I felt the power of God's Love
like a gently rushing river
going through every aspect
of my being.

What happened?
What did I do?

I simply stepped back,
put my ego aside,
and let God lead the way.

My Heart Sings

My heart sings out with joy
for the quietness of this moment.
At last, my heart and mind are vacant
of all thought but Yours.

Peace and tranquility abide everywhere,
and I know I need do nothing but be.

Loving

May our loving
   be like our breathing,
   smooth and easy,
   free flowing,
   effortless,
   continual,
   with no interruptions.

May we breathe in God's Limitless Love,
   so we can breathe out
   the boundless Love
   that is in our heart.

Children as Teachers of Peace

May the way to peace be paved by the
laughter and joy of children.

May the hands of children bridge all
countries into a world joined
in love, peace, and harmony.

May the trust and hope of all children,
wherever they may live, inspire us to
forgive and to forget and to love all
of our brothers and sisters with equal
and abundant love.

May children, as teachers of peace, lead
all of us to find the innocent child that
always remains in each of us so that
the world we see can be transformed
into a world of love that it was always
meant to be.

Becoming a Flower

What do you think would happen
   if even for one instant
   we would look at a flower
   and become that flower?

We would immediately know that we are here
   to reflect the indescribable, indefinable beauty
   of Our Creator's Love.

We would see ourselves as perfectly balanced
   with our function as giving this symbol
   of our love and beauty away.

We would see that flowers live in harmony
   with each other,
   at perfect peace.

Flowers, being God's Messengers of Love,
   have no attack thoughts, no guilty thoughts,
   and no thoughts of fighting
   and destroying each other.

continues

Flowers are truly a creation of God's Love
    here on earth.
They can only blossom and claim their beauty
    as accepting the Light from God's mind
    as an integral part of themselves.

Let us remind ourselves to become flowers and
    then give a flower to someone new each day.
Let us know that we are giving God's Love
    and our love as one away.
What a beautiful way to bring peace
    to ourselves and others.

Surrender

And I asked,
   "What is the secret of
   total surrender to Love?"

And I was told,
   The secret of surrender is simply
   not to think.
   It is letting perception gently
   dissolve into the knowledge of Love,
   the land of no change,
   the Kingdom of God.

   The secret of surrender is simply
   to do nothing and to be.

In the Stillness of This Moment

It is in the stillness of this moment that I
hear Your Voice ever present.

I experience no beginning and no ending,
no sense of time.

Left aside are all desires and any wishes
to achieve.

The dissolving of self into the Essence of
Your Being is the extension of Love
beyond, beyond, beyond.

On Meditation

What is meditation but an effort
    to experience God's Love.

It is getting away from the
    multitudinous thoughts and tensions
    of the unfinished business
    of our external life.

It is a willingness simply to be still
    and to listen.

Commitment

To be peaceful and joyful, there is but
    one commitment to make:

It is to live life, one second at a time,
    as if it is an eternal moment.

It is to make the decision,
    regardless of the behavior we observe,
    no matter where we are, or whom we are with,
    to be a vehicle of God's Perfect Love,
    to be totally accepting and defenseless,
    to give all of ourselves away in love,
    to give total, maximal, and unconditional love
    to everyone, excluding no one.

It is to make the commitment
    with every thought,
    with every breath,
    with every heartbeat.

It is to be helpful to those in need
    who are crying out for help and are
    suffering because of lack of love.

It is to make the decision
    to have the fire of compassion in our hearts
    to love the universe and all that is in it
    with tender loving care.

It is to make the decision to trust and accept
    God's boundless Love for ourselves, and
    thereby, become a Messenger of God's Love.

It is to demonstrate and teach only Love,
    for that is what we are.

I wrote this poem after returning from a visit to refugee camps in
Sudan in 1985 where there was much starvation and many deaths.
I learned a great deal about commitment from the many volunteers.

All That I Am

Oh Great Spirit of the Life Force of what I am,
    how grateful am I this day to have felt the
    omnipresence of Your Heart joined with mine.

How appreciative I am for feeling a touch of the
    peace and serenity, knowing that I am a part
    of all that is.

How blissful it is to know there is no end and no
    separation, that there is only Your Love which I am.

How beyond the words of beautiful, magnificent, and
    joyous, at their ultimate is the gift
    of them all blending into one
    that You gave me today.

Light on the Water

Luminescence from the sun, dancing with
the radiance of God, reminds me of
the ever presence of God's Love.

Let us take each other's hand and walk
toward the Light of God.

Let us stay in the presence of God and
in the nowness of joy.

Let us let go of separation of all kinds.

Let us resist the temptation to interpret
each other's behavior.

Let us stop our suffering.

Let us together, once and for all, let go of
all past hurts and unmet needs.

Let us put our total trust in God and then
see only the God Self in each other.

continues

Let us put all our faith in God and feel His
  Neverending Love fill us up to the brim.

Let us then let go of all self doubts and guilt
  that we have projected on to each other.

Let us fully trust ourselves because God is
  within us.

Let us join our will as one and let us be directed
  by God's Plan and not our own.

Every Step of the Way

To Age with Attitude
   is to age with grace
   and be positive about life.

It is to no longer see any value in
   hurting another person or yourself
   with words or with actions.

It is to consider that death
   is but an illusion and a doorway
   to Higher Consciousness.

Aging with Attitude
   is to be free of fear
   and making others wrong.

Aging with Attitude
   is another way
   of looking at the world.

It is to make forgiveness
   as important as breathing
   and to love all others
   as you would love yourself.

continues

113

Aging with Attitude celebrates love every
step of the way by living in the present and
choosing to be happy, peaceful, guiltless,
judgeless, and to be able to laugh at
yourself and the world you see.

The Great Awakening

It is the morning of Christ and
    the bells are ringing,
    music is in the air,
    roosters are crowing,
    dogs are barking,
    birds are singing and
    joy is everywhere.

The Great Awakening is here.
The end of fear, guilt, pain and anger is here.
The end of lamentations, despair,
    hopelessness, sacrifice, deprivation,
    death, and all illusions is here.

The Great Awakening is here.
The time of timelessness,
    the moment of total release and total
    freedom is here.
The Holy Instant of giving, of offering, of
    being awake in the Oneness of peace
    and love is here.

continues

The Great Awakening is here.
The moment of total and complete and
    everlasting love is here.
The Light is here, within us now
    and always, joining us with God and all
    Creation.

The Great Awakening is here.
It is a time of no time but the eternal now.
The Light and the Holy Instant are here
and the world and all that is in it is blessed
    with holiness and joy.

What is Beyond?

On this day the experience of my soul
    is beyond words.

What is beyond all feelings,
    beyond certainty and knowing
    that has no room for doubt?

What is beyond all limits
    and knows no barriers or boundaries?

What is beyond that which is
    all beautiful, magnificent and wonderful?

What is beyond the sunrise, the sunset,
    the moon and the sky?

What is beyond all feelings of love's abundance
    and having no needs?

What is beyond contentment,
    a feeling of well-being and
    total happiness and joy?

continues

What is beyond the splendor
  and the magic of nature?

What is beyond the fullness of Spirit
  that comes from the consciousness of giving?

What is beyond oneness, joining, and
  a state of no separation?

What is beyond feeling safe
  and knowing I will never
  be abandoned?

What is beyond the infinity of
  my passionate feelings of gratitude
  for all the love I continue to receive?

What is beyond awe,
  mystery and wonderment is
  God's Love for me
  and my love for God.

There Is Another Way

There is another way of being,
    another way of looking at the world.

There is a way of living in this world
    where we see that our function is to:
        love and to forgive,
        resist the temptation to judge anyone,
        let go of all guilt, blame, and fear,
        be helpful to others, and
        give love, rather than seek it.

We let go of our fear of death by knowing
    we are eternal, spiritual beings and that
    there is no death.

We heal our illusion that we are separate
    from God and each other.

Another way of living in this world is to know
    that Love will heal any and all problems
    that we might perceive we have.

It is to know that Love is the answer.

Infants' Eyes

Infants' eyes the world over,
how remarkably the same they are.
How full of trust and light they are
with their sparkle of joy and wonderment
and a neverending well of love
as you look inside.

But what absolutely fascinates me,
what softens, touches,
and completely opens my heart,
no matter where in the world I might be,
is the pure innocence
that is always in
an infant's eyes.

My Fight with God Is Over

My hand stretches out to God
and my fight with God is over.
My fists have transformed
into open and empty palms.
The past and all my attachments
have disappeared into the mist.

I have awakened from
my dream of separation
and I know God is within me
as I am within God.

God has never left me
and is my only true relationship.

The Peace of God

The Peace of God is the stillness of the night.
It is the gentle sounds of the surf hugging the shore.
It is the sun shining through the fog in the morning.
It is the joyful laughter of children throughout the world.

The Peace of God is the Love
    which obliterates all fears and separateness.
It is being whole and one with life.

The Peace of God is our only true identity.
It is our Light reflecting God's Presence here on earth.
It is that eternal state of bliss
    that transcends all of our physical experiences.
Its extension is beyond what we can imagine.

The Peace of God is the everlasting flow of God's Love,
    moving through us and gently unfolding on itself.
It is our gratitude for the Love God created in us.

Home is Just Around the Corner

Home is just around the corner.
Our journey is about to end.

The dream of separation is about
    to vanish, as we remember
    our Source of Eternal Love.

Jesus, At Last I Have Found You

Oh Jesus, my Elder Brother, you have been here,
    within my still mind all the time.
It was but my guilt and fear that kept Your Presence
    hidden from me.

Your Quiet Certainty, Your Gentleness, Your Song of
    Unending Love resonates in my heart as an ancient
    melody that makes all creation dance with joy.

You have touched me, and I feel the abundance of
    God's Love within me and within everything I see.
The sky is bluer, the mountains more majestic,
    the trees more serene, the ocean more gentle, and
    the Light of Christ is shining in everyone I behold.

Oh Jesus, my Dear Brother, My Savior, the completion
    of myself, You have touched me and purified my
    thoughts and my heart.

You have touched me and made me free of my physical
    identity.
You have touched me and for this everlasting instant,
    I am once again free.
    I am free of all illusions.
    I am free of fear.
    I am free of guilt.

I am free of pain.
    I am free of all problems, of all questions
    and concerns about tomorrow.

You have touched me and for this eternal instant
    every aspect of myself knows that there is only
    joy in the now, there is only peace in the now,
    there is only love in the now.

Oh Jesus, my Beloved Teacher, I release all.
    I let go of all.
I come toward God with empty hands and
    complete myself with You.

Oh dear Jesus, my Beloved Brother, I know that
    all I need do is be.
I thank you for Your patience.
The essence of my being is full of joy and laughter,
    as the song of gratitude continues to resonate
    from my heart to God, to myself, and to all of
    God's Creation.

Thank you, Jesus. Thank you. Thank you.
I will never walk alone again.

When We Teach Only Love

Each of us can make a difference
    when we teach only love, not fear,
    when we put an end to indifference and
    when we let go of selfish needs.

Each of us can make a difference
    when we teach only love,
    when we awaken each day
    by showing each other the way

Each of us can make a difference
    when we teach only love,
    when we commit ourselves to have a heart
    that beats only with compassion,
    where caring for one another becomes
    our only passion.

Each of us can make a difference
    when we teach only love,
    when giving, kindness, patience, gratitude
    and tenderness are the way that we pray.

When Love and Forgiveness become
    our song of the day.

Each of us can make a difference
   when we teach only love,
   when everything we think, say, and do
   becomes our gift of love to God.

Each of us can make a difference
   when we teach only love,
   when we commit our lives to joy,
   when we commit our hearts to peace.

Each of us can make a difference
   when we teach only love.

Avery's Passion for Life

When my grand nephew Avery was four, we took a walk. He stopped, got on his knees to examine a weed and looked at it for a long time, as if he were taking in every part of it. Then he very gently pulled it out of the ground, smelled it, tasted it, and then gave it to me, saying with all the passion of his tiny being, "Isn't this the most beautiful thing you've ever seen?"

Spiritual teachers come in all sizes, some of them quite small. Young children remind us to bring passion and appreciation to each moment and to remember that the present is the only time we can consciously live in.

Rushing through life to get to a future that will always be ahead of us or regretting a past that's over and can't be undone, causes us to lose sight of the now, which is the only real time in our lives.

The Fishing Pole

Instead of sitting in my office for counseling sessions, many of the children I saw were more relaxed and open to talking when they fished with me on the dock next to my office. Because one boy enjoyed fishing so much, I gave him a fishing pole for his 10th birthday.

Thirty-three years later, when my wife and I met with an illustrator for her up-coming book, I was surprised to find the illustrator was the same person who had been my young patient all those years ago. We spent two hours talking with him, his wife, and two children.

When we were about to leave, he asked me to wait a minute because he wanted to show me something. After a few minutes, he returned holding the small fishing pole I'd given him all those years ago. Without saying a word, he reached out and handed it to me. Tears came to my eyes as I recognized how important our relationship had been to him. He was a teacher, coming back into my life to remind me of the power of what I'd thought was merely a simple act of kindness.

Bobby's Deathbed Wisdom

When I visited Bobby, a fourteen-year-old boy who was dying of cancer, I saw that he was pale and motionless. I sat down by his bed and held his hand for a while. Then I asked him if he would like to talk into a tape recorder to tell his experience with cancer and give his advice to other kids who also have this disease.

Much to my amazement, Bobby sat up and opened his eyes and took the tape recorder. As he spoke, the blood came back into his face and his pallor disappeared. He talked for about ten minutes, and everything he said was important and helpful. But what I remember most was his statement, "Tell all those kids and adults you see to remember that their purpose in life—no matter what shape their body is in and as long as they are breathing—is to love and help others."

A Friend and a Teacher

Arnie and I were roommates throughout medical school. At the time, I didn't realize that we would remain lifelong friends or that he would help me learn what friendship was really about.

Soon after graduation, Arnie became ill with polio and remained a quadriplegic for the rest of his life. In spite of his extreme physical limitation, he became a psychiatrist, a full professor at U.C.L.A. and an author. While Arnie didn't profess to be religious, there was a Light to him that was obvious to everyone. People were affected by his quiet spirituality.

Despite his paralysis, Arnie gave me so much more than I could ever give him. Through the example of the way he lived his life, he taught me not to feel sorry for myself, never to give up, to always persevere, and to know that there will always be a solution.

There was nothing we couldn't tell each other because we knew we wouldn't be judged. He taught me the power of humor and hope in the healing process and that when you're helping another, which he spent his life doing, you're also helping yourself.

continues

Above all, Arnie taught me that the only thing that really matters in life is love. Perhaps the most important aspect of our relationship was expressed by the silence of our love and appreciation, the softness we could see in each other's eyes, and the knowledge that we would always be there for one another.

Deep friendship is the home of love, trust, honesty, faith, and the freedom to be ourselves at our craziest moments, yet still know that we'll be accepted and loved as we are.

A Message for Chanukah for My Parents

You are grandparents, and see yourselves as old.
Close your eyes to time and know that you are
    everything that is ageless.

You are love, joy and peace all melted into one.

Know that life and death are not finite.

Let your fears slip gently away.
Know that your loneliness and your isolation,
    your feelings of desperation, and your fear of
    separation are but part of a passing nightmare.

Wake up with your children and your
    children's children, and see yourself
    as one with all that is.

Wake up and know that you are limitless love
    and eternal life made into one.

Let the light of God erase the wrinkles of pain,
    fear, and loneliness from your face.

continues

And let your smile of joy and eternal bliss
light up the road so that the whole world
can see its way to its forgotten home.

Dad

Dad, although you are no longer here in physical form,
   I do feel your presence all about me.

As I look at my flowers and plants and love them, I am
   grateful for your teaching me to love the earth and
   all that grows from it.

As I look at nature I feel your presence nearby, and I
   remember you opening my heart to the harmony,
   balance and interconnectedness of nature.

Dad, patience and gentleness are high priorities of your
   character, and I would like your help because
   I am still having problems here.

There are many days I find myself not being
   very gentle or patient with myself or others.
   I long to model myself after you because
   I know that our minds are still joined,
   and I know that you can still help me here.

Dad, please hear my willingness to have your thoughts
   fill my mind so that I may become a teacher of God
   and learn to be gentle and patient too.

continues

My son, there is nothing to learn because
  your natural state and that of all your brothers and
  sisters is patience and gentleness because as
  God's Creations, your attributes
  are the same as His.

We can only be gentle when we are free from
  the fear of possible attack.

We can only be gentle when we see only love.
And when we choose to see only love, it is
  only love that we will find.

See only the light about you and in all others.

Know that you are the light and that there is
nothing you can do to put out that light;
  all that you can do is to hide the light from yourself
  by accepting fear rather than love.

The light you are is innocence; it is gentleness;
  it is love.

Patience comes from knowing without any doubt that
  there are no problems, there is no separation, and
  that we are all joined in Love,
  in Oneness with God
  and each other.

When you are living in the illusory world,
   patience is the ability to wait without fear
   and without anxiety and with only love
   because you are sure that the outcome
   is an awakening of our being joined with God.

Patience comes from letting go of experiencing
   the physical world as being real.

And above all, patience means letting God's Plan
   unfold as the only Plan; it is this that is
   causing you difficulty today.

My son, ask yourself if you truly want to surrender
   to God. If the answer is yes, patience and
   gentleness will fill your being this instant.

Message to My Sons

My sons, I see you as one.
You are my heart and soul
    wrapped into one.

You are my teacher of patience
    and trust, and love and joy.

You are the knowledge and the
    truth that dissolves experience.

You are the light that lets time and age,
    and pain and guilt disappear.

You are the moon and sun combined
    into one pure light.

My sons, it is with loving gratitude that
    I thank you for teaching me that you
    are only love, and that my essence
    is but a reflection of you.

To My Granddaughter
August 26, 1986

Dear Jacquelyn Amour Jampolsky,

I write this letter to you the night after I held you in my arms, while I am flying on an airplane to the Soviet Union to an international meeting on Children's Peace and Health Education.

I would like to try to share with you what went on in my heart as I held you. I have heard the word "bliss" many times in my life, never knowing for sure what that word meant. But last night no one had to tell me what that word meant for I experienced in your presence, pure bliss.

At 22 days of age, you are a bundle of pure light, love and joy. You are more than just your body; to me, you are a powerhouse of loving energy that filled my heart, the room and the world with love.

The day I saw you I was running around taking care of last minute errands before leaving on my journey. When I came to see you, I was still carrying some tensions of the day, and just being with you rounded out the sharp corners that I was carrying within me.

continues

Why should holding you have such a profound effect on me? I think it was your innocence and your complete trust. It was not what you did, it was your Being - radiating all of creation's love and light through your tiny body. I was sure that no matter what problem, what pain, what illness anyone had, just by holding you and feeling your unconditional love that they would be healed.

I have never seen your mother and father happier as they played and talked with you. Oh, I forgot to mention that I think there is something very special about your, and all babies' smell. Perhaps it is the reflection of all the newness and the freshness of your Being because to me you were like a breath of fresh air—wiping out the past and reminding me that this is the only moment there is, a moment of and for love.

Jacquelyn Amour, I want to thank you for coming into this world and choosing to be an Angel of Light. I want to thank you for the miracle of love that you bring with you to heal the earth and the universe. I am so grateful for your softness and gentleness, your innocence and for your trust and for reminding me that everything I see in you is but a reflection of what is in me.

I do believe that if all the grandparents of the world would have the opportunity of not only holding their own grandchild, but of holding infants from all the countries in the world, there could never be a rationalization or justification for war, or for hurting anyone ever again.

I want to also tell you that I had a phone call from a friend in the East who wanted my help. I talked to her on the phone while I was lying down on the floor, and when I finished the phone call, your father put you on my chest while I was still lying on the floor. You cooed and went to sleep with your face on my neck. Your mother and father said that they had never seen me happier and they were right.

As we grow older, many of us, like myself, are tempted to forget who we are and what our purpose is.

Please let me be your witness so that you may never doubt the power of creation's love and light that is within you, and always remember that nothing can ever turn out that eternal light that is the essence of your Being.

May you continue to remind yourself that your presence here is to heal the planet by letting your light and love shine on all your sisters and brothers

continues

and on all living things. May you continue to trust and have faith in the Creative Love Force of the world and be always a messenger of God's Love by continuing to give your unconditional love to everyone, excluding no one; and may you continue to share your happiness and joy with the world.

With boundless gratitude and love for your Being,

Grampa Jerry

Brother Swan

Let us forget the dark and hurtful ways
We travelled on with you; the twisted feet
That walked against the holy Will of God,
Away from peace and from the quiet lake
That was the resting place that He ordained.
The fumbling, failing creature has become
The gift of God. In holy thankfulness
We see in you what each of us can be
And will become with you. You chose for us,
And turned your bleeding feet the other way,
And we give thanks to you who chose for us.
So let us look with wonder on the swan,
The gift of God, the holy light of Christ,
Resplendent in his shining sinlessness.
The purity of Heaven is your gift.

Let us receive it now in thankfulness,
For your release. Your free, unfettered wings
Remind us that your freedom is our own,
Remind us that our freedom is of God.

My dearest of friends, Dr. Helen Schucman, scribe of
A Course in Miracles, wrote this poem for my 51st birthday,
February 11, 1976, at the request of Judith Skutch Whitson.

A Message for Helen, Loving Scribe of *A Course in Miracles*
November 13, 1976

Loving scribe, who has faithfully carried out the job
    that was assigned, your work is almost done.
Your gift of patience is asked an instant more.
The last flicker of the flame of doubt is about to go out.

The Eternal Light of Love is about to shine through the
    last cloud on the horizon.
The Lily of Eternal Love is about to blossom
    in blazing glory.
The final awakening from your dream is but
    an instant away.

Time is about to stop.

Your present uneasiness is only the ego's last breath
    of awareness
    that the beginning and the end are but the same.
The Constant Echo of Love becomes the mirror of
    yourself as you leave the world behind.
Roses permeate the air and tell you that your home,
    the Kingdom of God, is but a step away.

Your brothers and sisters are grateful for your being.

We thank you,
    loving scribe, and God blesses you
    for lighting the way to the memory and
    knowledge that your Older Brother, you,
    and all of your brothers and sisters are one.

Thank you for your amazing commitment for
    being the scribe of
    A Course in Miracles.

SPIRITUAL REMINDERS

As it takes only one speck of dirt
to destroy the purity of clear water,
it takes but one speck of fear to hide
the presence of Love.

I learned today that when my chest
feels like it is in a vise and
my breathing is tight, I have
inside tears.

The voice of Love is more easily heard
when my mind is still.

To the ego, life is a game of hide-and-seek.
We hide the love that is within us from ourselves
and then we seek it outside ourselves,
where it can never be found.

I know that projection is a mirror, not a fact,
but when I am fearful, I am stuck in my ego,
and everything I see in the world
looks very real to me.

Possessiveness is the heart of the ego,
which is limitless in its desire
to control both people and things.

We will truly have more peaceful relationships
when we tear up all of our scripts for others.

A heart that is full of God's Love
is a heart that
is never in need of anything.

Jealousy is an accomplice of the ego
that turns the illusion of love into hate.

All prejudice and discrimination is
reversible because all of it comes from fear.

Have you ever found, like me,
that when you were stuck
in your head,
it was music that set you free?

When I am depressed,
and living my life
in the quicksand of my ego,
somewhere deep inside,
I know
that I am denying
the Presence of God.

My ego says that I have no right to be happy.
I deserve to suffer, and there is no way
to get rid of guilt because I am sinful.
May this be the time that I heal myself
by saying good-bye to my fearful ego.

The nightmares of my life seem to disappear
as soon as I stop interpreting
other people's behavior
and remember that we are all
One with Our Creator.

Egos love to worry about future and past events,
and worry leads to deeper fears
which, in turn, lead to more worry.

It becomes easier to forgive
when we choose to no longer
believe that we are victims.

Our egos want to control and direct every situation.
This is a given.
If we hope to access Inner Guidance,
it's most helpful
to come with empty hands,
holding on to nothing.

How deceived was I to think that what I feared
was in the world instead of in my mind.

Perhaps the biggest gift that humankind
has been given
is the choice to decide what thoughts and attitudes
we put in our minds.

Whether we live our lives filled with
peace or conflict
is ultimately determined by our attitudes.

Many things that look like limitations and disabilities,
such as my dyslexia, I now look on
as a blessing in disguise.

Perceiving ourselves as "not good enough"
stunts our growth in the present,
which has nothing to do with the past,
and keeps us feeling limited and unfulfilled.

When I open my heart to God's Love,
any need I thought I had disappears.

The way to Peace is to stop worrying
and put the future in the hands of God.

The way of the ego is to have us forget about God
by getting and attaching ourselves
to people and things.
The way of the Spirit is to have us remember God
by having no attachments and giving our Love
to everyone unconditionally.

Perhaps true healing has more to do with listening
with unconditional love than with trying
to fix people up.

Love is listening and listening is Love.

Freedom comes when I trust My Creator
to be My Friend.

Spirit, speak to me of My Identity.
You are pure Love; you are Me.
At last you have discovered how to see.
All that you need ever do is to be.

Please help me to awaken from my dreams.
Let me look into the mirror and see myself
as I truly am,
as a Reflection of Your Love.

Forgiveness is the shortest route to God.

Man's law is that when you go faster,
you get somewhere.
God's Law is that when you go slower,
you go farther
and that when you stop going and remain still,
you are there.

When given with love, the smallest gift has
transformative power.
And when accompanied
by a hug, it can be magical.

Forgiveness is the eraser
that makes the hurtful past disappear.

Perhaps one of the most important things that I have come to know after these many decades of working with people is that, ultimately, I do not know what is best for another person.

I think that the most important equation in the world
is that the fullness of one's heart is directly
proportional to how much love one gives.

Nothing real can be threatened.
Nothing unreal exists.
Herein lies the Peace of God.

From the Introduction of *A Course in Miracles*

AUTHOR'S NOTE

Forgiveness has been one of the most important lessons that I have had to learn to live a life based on love. I have found that forgiveness can release us from the past and deliver us to the joy of living fully in this moment. It stops our inner battles with ourselves and allows us to stop recycling anger and blame. Forgiveness is the great healer that allows us to feel joined and at one with each other and all that is life.

Forgiveness, though, is not one of those things which we ever complete in our lives. It is ongoing, always a work in progress. It is a never-ending process, because as long as we are living in these bodies there is a part of us that is going to be tempted, again and again, to make judgments. However, because of the freedom we come to know when we forgive ourselves and others, we learn to recognize when we're slipping back to blame and judgment, and we can choose to stop ourselves. Forgiveness opens the door to hearing the Voice of God, guiding us through our lives.

Diane and I gave a workshop titled "Forgiveness and Reconciliation for Religious Leaders" in Bosnia in 1998. It was the first gathering of its kind since the end of the horrendous war. Workshop representatives were from Croatia, Bosnia, and Serbia, all a part of the former Yugoslavia. Needless to say, many of them did not want to even be in the same room with the others. All of them had encountered much suffering and pain themselves, along with those they served. Tensions were high, grudges long, and forgiveness was feeling far out of reach.

We asked them if they would all pray with us and ask for guidance as to how best to proceed toward a place of healing, where we could find some common ground. Reluctantly, they consented to do so.

After a very long silence, a young man, about thirty years of age, began to rise and stand quietly in place. He began to speak softly and share his journey. He had lived in the countryside with his parents, grandparents, and four younger siblings. He had been away from their home, serving in the military, and the day he returned, he found the house boarded up with the doors and windows nailed shut. The house was in raging flames, and his entire family was inside being burned to death. He heard the screams, but it was impossible to free them.

He stood there in shock and rage, and one thing became crystal clear to him. He shared with us that at that moment in time, he knew he had to make a choice. He was either going to spend the rest of his life hunting down the men that murdered his whole family....or he was going to have to find a way to forgive. The young man was now a priest, devoting his life to love and forgiveness.

The telling of an extraordinary story that day, literally, opened hearts, changed minds, and deepened compassion in the recognition that everyone there had suffered and lost so much. As has happened numerous times in our life and work together, Diane and I witnessed a miracle that day, one that Bill Thetford describes as...*a shift in perception that removes the blocks to the awareness of Love's Presence in our lives.*

On the following pages, I share with you my poem, "Forgiveness, The Greatest Healer of All," which I was inspired to write that day.

Forgiveness, The Greatest Healer of All

To forgive is the prescription
   for happiness.

To not forgive is the prescription
   to suffer.

Is it possible
   all pain regardless of its cause
   has some component of
   un-forgiveness in it?

To hold on to vengeful thoughts,
   to withhold our love and compassion
   certainly must interfere
   with our health
   and our immune system.

Holding on to what we call
   justified anger
   interferes with our experiencing
   the Peace of God.

To forgive
   does not mean
   agreeing with the act;
   it does not mean condoning
   an outrageous behavior.

Forgiveness means
   no longer living in
   the fearful past.

Forgiveness means
   no longer scratching the wounds
   so they continue to bleed.

Forgiveness means
   living and loving
   completely in the present,
   without the shadows of the past.

Forgiveness means
   freedom from anger
   and attack thoughts.

continues

Forgiveness means
    letting go of all hopes
    for a better past.

Forgiveness means
    not excluding
    your love from anyone.

Forgiveness means
    healing the hole in your heart
    caused by unforgiving thoughts.

Forgiveness means
    seeing the Light of God
    in everyone, regardless
    of their behavior.

Forgiveness is not just for
    the other person – but for ourselves
    the mistakes we have made,
    and the guilt and shame we still hold onto.

Forgiveness in the deepest sense
   is forgiving ourselves
   for separating ourselves from a loving God.

Forgiveness means
   forgiving God and our
   possible misperceptions of God
   that we have ever been
   abandoned or left alone.

To forgive this very instant
   means no longer being
   King or Queen of the Procrastinator's Club.

Forgiveness opens the door
   for us to feel joined with Spirit
   and at one with everyone with God.

It is never too early
   to forgive.
It is never too late
   to forgive.

continues

How long does it take
  to forgive?
  It depends on your belief system.

If you believe it will never happen,
  it will never happen.

If you believe it will take six months,
  it will take six months.

If you believe it will take but a second,
  that's all that it will take.

I believe with all my heart
  that peace will come to the world
  when each of us takes the
  responsibility of forgiving everyone,
  including ourselves, completely.

ABOUT THE AUTHOR

Gerald Jampolsky, M.D. is a Child and Adult
Psychiatrist and graduate of Stanford University
School of Medicine. In 1975, along with others, he
founded the first Center for Attitudinal Healing, in
Tiburon, California. Now, there are independent
Centers throughout the world, on five continents
and in dozens of countries, all offering free support
services for children, adolescents and adults.
Attitudinal Healing continues to be adapted for use
in just about every aspect of our lives.

Dr. Jampolsky is a member of the adjunct faculty
of the University of Hawaii School of Medicine,
Department of Complementary and Alternative
Medicine. He has authored and co-authored several
bestselling books. Over the last four decades, he
and his wife, Diane Cirincione, Ph.D., have been

invited to work together in over 60 countries and are recipients of numerous international awards.

In 2005, Dr. Jampolsky received the Excellence in Medicine—Pride in the Profession Award from the American Medical Association for his lifetime humanitarian service and for his contribution of Attitudinal Healing to the field of health.

In 2015, both Drs. Jampolsky and Cirincione were awarded the Ellis Island Medals of Honor for living lives dedicated to helping others and sharing their personal and professional gifts for the benefit of humanity.

For more information visit:
www.AHInternational.org
You may also write to:
Attitudinal Healing International
3001 Bridgeway, Suite K-368
Sausalito, California, U.S.A. 94965
Tel: 877-244-3392

Books by the Author

Love is Letting Go of Fear

Teach Only Love: The Twelve Principles of Attitudinal Healing

Good-Bye to Guilt: Releasing Fear Through Forgiveness

Forgiveness: The Greatest Healer of All

Out of Darkness, Into the Light: A Journey of Inner Healing

Shortcuts to God: Finding Peace Quickly Through Practical Spirituality

One Person Can Make a Difference: Ordinary People Doing Extraordinary Things

The "Oh Shit" Factor: Waste Management for Our Minds

Books with Diane Cirincione, Ph.D.

A Mini Course for Life

Love is the Answer: Creating Positive Relationships

Change Your Mind, Change Your Life

Wake-up Calls

*Finding Our Way Home: Spiritual Stories That
Ignite Our Spiritual Core*

Simple Thoughts That Can Change Your Life

Me First and the Gimme Gimmes

Aging With Attitude

Books with Lee Jampolsky, Ph.D.

*Listen to Me: A Book for Women and Men About
Father-Son Relationships*

Made in the USA
Middletown, DE
10 November 2017